SO-EIC-455

AMERICA'S
PRESIDENTS
ACTIVITY • FUN BOOK

Incorporated

COPYRIGHT ©1988 ELVIRA GAMIELLO AND KIDSBOOKS, INC.
KIDSBOOKS, INC., 7004 N. CALIFORNIA AVE., CHICAGO, ILL. 60645, U.S.A.
ALL RIGHTS RESERVED   MANUFACTURED IN U.S.A.
ISBN 0-942025-51-2

ON APRIL 30, 1789, GEORGE WASHINGTON BECAME THE FIRST PRESIDENT OF THE UNITED STATES. WHERE WAS HE SWORN IN?

USE THIS CHART TO DECODE THE ANSWER.

A	B	C	D	E	F	G	H	I	J	K	L	M
14	9	26	11	4	1	20	7	16	3	21	13	24

N	O	P	Q	R	S	T	U	V	W	X	Y	Z
23	17	6	22	12	19	10	15	5	25	2	8	18

___ ___ ___ ___   ___ ___ ___ ___
26 16 10 8   7   14 13 13

___ ___
16 23

___ ___ ___   ___ ___ ___ ___ .
23 4   25   8   17 12 21

SEE ANSWER SECTION

2

WHEN WASHINGTON
RETIRED IN 1796,
JOHN ADAMS WAS
ELECTED THE
NATION'S SECOND
PRESIDENT OVER
THOMAS JEFFERSON.
WHAT WAS UNIQUE
ABOUT THE ADAMS
LIVING QUARTERS?

1797   1801

TO FIND OUT, FILL IN THE BLANK SPACES WITH
THEIR CORRECT MISSING VOWELS A·E·I·O·U.

TH_ _D_MS
F_M_LY W_S
TH_ F_RST
F_M_LY T_
L_V_ _N TH_
WH_T_ H__S_.

SEE ANSWER SECTION

3

1801   1809

POPULARLY KNOWN AS
THE AUTHOR OF THE
DECLARATION OF
INDEPENDENCE,
THOMAS JEFFERSON
WAS OUR 3RD
PRESIDENT. DURING
HIS TERM, THE COUNTRY
DOUBLED IN SIZE WHEN
THE LOUISIANA TERRITORY WAS
PURCHASED FROM FRANCE.
WHAT DID JEFFERSON INVENT
THAT IS STILL USED TODAY?

CORRECTLY ANSWER EACH CLUE. WRITE THE
CIRCLED LETTERS IN NUMERICAL ORDER TO
COMPLETE THE ANSWER.

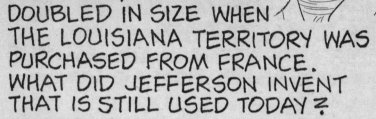

Clue	Answer
THE DAY AFTER MONDAY	◯5 _ _ ◯11 ◯6 ◯3 ◯18
NOT LOUD	_ ◯14 ◯1 ◯10
SUMMER MONTH	◯12 ◯17 _ _ ◯4 _
UNITED STATES OF _____	◯15 ◯13 _ ◯8 ◯2 _ ◯7
FROZEN WATER	_ ◯16 ◯9

THE D_C_M_L _YS_EM OF
  1 2 3   4   5
OLL _ _S AND C_N_ _ USED IN
6   7 8   9 10 11
_ _ER_C_N _ _RRENC_ .
12 13 14 15   16 17   18

SEE ANSWER SECTION

JAMES MADISON, THE 4TH PRESIDENT, BROUGHT THE U.S. A VICTORY IN THE WAR OF 1812. HIS "FIRST LADY" DOLLY MADISON, INTRODUCED ICE CREAM TO WHITE HOUSE GUESTS. PRIOR TO HIS TERM, HE WAS INVOLVED IN THE MAKING OF THE CONSTITUTION — WHAT TITLE WAS HE GIVEN?

1809   1817

EACH WORD CAN BE TURNED INTO THE NAME OF A COLOR BY CHANGING ONE LETTER. AFTER DOING THIS PLACE THE CIRCLED LETTERS IN NUMERICAL ORDER TO COMPLETE THE ANSWER.

BLOCK	_ _ Ⓞ _ _
	1
WHILE	_ Ⓞ Ⓞ Ⓞ _
	4 8 6
PINE	_ _ Ⓞ Ⓞ _
	7 5
ROD	Ⓞ _ _
	3
GREED	_ _ _ Ⓞ Ⓞ
	2 9

"F_TH_ _ OF T_E
   1   2 3   4
CO_S_ _TUT_O_"
   5 6 7   8 9

SEE ANSWER SECTION   5

JAMES MONROE, WHO HAD
SERVED AS SECRETARY
OF WAR UNDER MADISON,
BECAME OUR 5TH
PRESIDENT. HIS
MONROE DOCTRINE
BECAME A BASIC
PART OF AMERICAN
INTERNATIONAL
DIPLOMACY. HOW MANY
TERMS DID HE SERVE
AS PRESIDENT?

TO FIND OUT, FILL IN ALL THE
AREAS THAT CONTAIN THE LETTER "M".

1817   1825

SEE ANSWER SECTION

JOHN QUINCY ADAMS,
OUR 6TH PRESIDENT,
DREW UP A PROGRAM
TO FURTHER THE ARTS
AND SCIENCES. DURING
HIS TERM HE ALSO
IMPROVED THE
EDUCATIONAL SYSTEM.
WHO WAS HIS FATHER?

TO ANSWER THIS QUESTION,
FILL IN THE BLANKS WITH THEIR
CORRECT MISSING VOWELS —
A·E·I·O·U.

1825   1829

HIS FATHER
WAS THE
NATION'S
SECOND
PRESIDENT,
JOHN ADAMS.

SEE ANSWER SECTION

ANDREW JACKSON, OUR 7TH PRESIDENT, WAS A MILITARY HERO DURING THE WAR OF 1812. HE WAS KNOWN AS "OLD HICKORY" FOR HIS TOUGHNESS. WHAT FAMOUS FRONTIERSMAN DID HE FIGHT ALONGSIDE WITH?

1829   1837

CROSS OUT ALL THE LETTERS THAT APPEAR 3 TIMES, WRITE THE REMAINING LETTERS, AS THEY APPEAR, IN THE SPACES BELOW.

F	D	A	N	M
V	G	B	Y	C
N	R	M	G	O
C	S	K	N	B
B	G	F	E	S
F	T	M	S	T

_ _ _ _ _

_ _ _ _ _ _ _ _ _

8

SEE ANSWER SECTION

MARTIN VAN BUREN
LED A HARD PRESIDENTIAL
CAMPAIGN BEFORE
DEFEATING HARRISON
TO BECOME OUR 8TH
PRESIDENT. HIS TERM
WAS PLAGUED WITH A
DEPRESSION THAT HIT
THE NATION IN 1837.
HIS CAMPAIGN NICKNAME
"OLD KINDERHOOK"
GAVE THE COUNTRY WHAT
POPULAR EXPRESSION ?

1837   1841

FIND AND CIRCLE THE WORDS FROM THIS LIST
IN THE PUZZLE BELOW. WRITE THE LETTERS THAT
ARE NOT USED IN THE BLANK SPACES.

BRAVE • DEBT • FEDERAL • FLAG • FREE •
LAW • ORDER • PEACE • POWER • TERM • WIN •

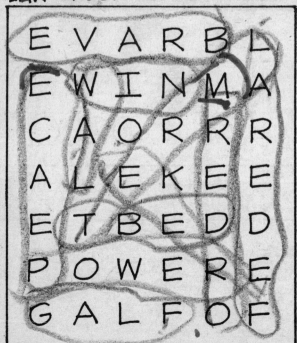

```
E V A R B L
E W I N M A
C A O R R R
A L E K E E
E T B E D D
P O W E R E
G A L F O F
```

" — • — • "

WILLIAM HENRY HARRISON'S TERM AS OUR 9TH PRESIDENT WAS CUT SHORT BY HIS DEATH ONE MONTH AFTER HIS INAUGURATION. HE WAS ELECTED USING THE POPULAR SLOGAN "TIPPECANOE AND TYLER TOO." WHY WAS HE KNOWN AS "TIPPECANOE"?

1841

WRITE THE OPPOSITE OF EACH WORD AND PLACE THE CIRCLED LETTERS IN THEIR CORRECT NUMERICAL ORDER TO COMPLETE THE ANSWER.

UP	◯◯ _ ◯
	8 4 7
COLD	◯◯◯
	3 15 11
LEFT	_ ◯ _ ◯
	6 2
SIT	◯◯◯◯ _
	9 13 1 14
SHORT	_ ◯◯◯
	10 5 12

FOR HIS DEFE _ _ OF _ _ STI _ E
        1 2   3 4   5

_ _ _ IAN _ AT THE B _ _ T _ E
6 7 8   9   10 11   12

OF _ IPPECA _ _ E RIVER.
  13   14 15

SEE ANSWER SECTION

JOHN TYLER WAS OUR 10TH PRESIDENT AND WAS RESPONSIBLE FOR TEXAS BEING ADMITTED TO THE UNION. HE WAS THE FIRST TO BECOME PRESIDENT BY SUCCESSION. WHAT WAS UNIQUE ABOUT TYLER'S FAMILY?

USE THIS SPECIAL CHART TO DECODE THE ANSWER.

A	B	C	D	E	F	G	H
•	•|	|•	••	••|	|••	•|•	•••

I	J	K	L	M	N	O	P
•••|	|•••	|•••|	••|••	•|•|	|•|	|••|	•||

Q	R	S	T	U	V	W	X	Y	Z
••||	•••||	||•	|||••	|||•••	•|•|	•|••	•••|•	•||•	••|••

JAMES KNOX POLK, OUR 11ᵀᴴ PRESIDENT, MADE GREAT ACHIEVEMENTS DURING HIS TERM. HE RESTORED AN INDEPENDENT U.S. TREASURY AND ACQUIRED CALIFORNIA. HOW WAS CALIFORNIA OBTAINED?

1845

1849

CROSS OUT ALL THE LETTERS THAT HAVE A BOX □. WRITE THE REMAINING LETTERS, AS THEY APPEAR IN THE BLANK SPACES

N	M	E	I
X	D	H	T
L	I	C	A
W	N	S	W
A	O	R	N

THROUGH THE

— — — — — — —

— — — .

SEE ANSWER SECTION

ZACHARY TAYLOR'S POPULARITY AS A WAR HERO ELECTED HIM OUR 12TH PRESIDENT. HE WAS NICKNAMED "OLD ROUGH AND READY". WHERE WAS TAYLOR WHEN HE SUFFERED A SUNSTROKE AND FOOD POISONING AND ULTIMATELY DIED?

FOLLOW THE PATH TO THE CORRECT ANSWER.

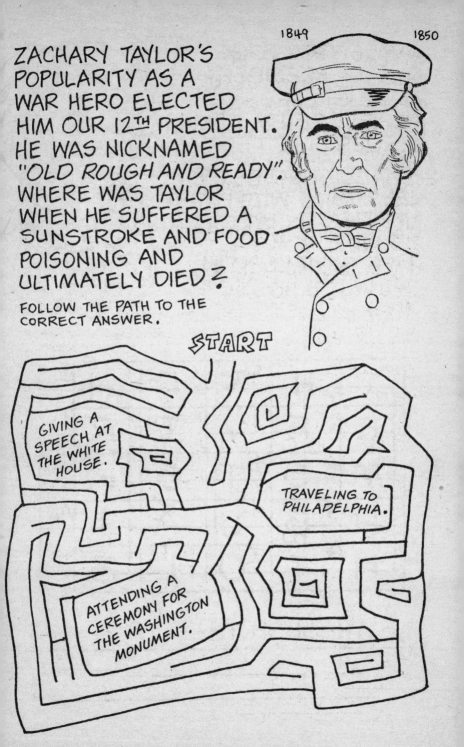

1849

1850

START

GIVING A SPEECH AT THE WHITE HOUSE.

TRAVELING TO PHILADELPHIA.

ATTENDING A CEREMONY FOR THE WASHINGTON MONUMENT.

SEE ANSWER SECTION

MILLARD FILLMORE, OUR 13TH PRESIDENT, OPPOSED FEDERAL BILLS CONCERNING SLAVERY. HE ESTABLISHED BETTER RELATIONS WITH LATIN AMERICA. WHAT DID HIS WIFE, ABIGAIL, HAVE INSTALLED IN THE WHITE HOUSE?

1850   1853

CIRCLE THE EVEN NUMBERED LETTERS AND WRITE THEM IN THE BLANK SPACES.

10 T	5 H	9 R	7 D	2 H
4 E	14 F	15 V	18 I	4 R
1 M	12 S	16 T	17 S	5 R
13 H	8 B	3 J	10 A	6 T
2 H	6 T	12 U	11 L	8 B

___ ___ ___   ___ ___ ___ ___

___ ___ ___ ___ ___ ___ ___ ___ .

SEE ANSWER SECTION

FRANKLIN PIERCE, OUR 14TH PRESIDENT, WAS A BRIGADIER GENERAL IN THE MEXICAN WAR. AS PRESIDENT, HE AGREED TO THE KANSAS-NEBRASKA ACT WHICH LET SETTLERS DECIDE ON SLAVE OR FREE STATUS. HE WAS THE SECOND YOUNGEST CANDIDATE TO BE ELECTED PRESIDENT. HOW OLD WAS HE?

1853   1857

FILL IN THE AREAS THAT CONTAIN A "P" TO FIND OUT.

SEE ANSWER SECTION

JAMES BUCHANAN, AS OUR 15TH PRESIDENT, MADE EVERY EFFORT TO DEAL WITH THE ISSUE OF SLAVERY. HE BEGAN TO NOTICE THE SEPARATION OF IDEALS BETWEEN THE NORTHERN AND SOUTHERN STATES. WHAT NEW TYPE OF MESSENGER SERVICE RAN SUCCESSFULLY BETWEEN 1860-1861?

1857   1861

TO FIND OUT, WRITE THESE WORDS IN THEIR CORRECT SPACES. THEN WRITE THE CIRCLED LETTERS IN THEIR CORRECT NUMERICAL ORDER.

EXECUTIVE • PATRIOT • PIONEER • PRESIDENT • STATE • YOUNG •

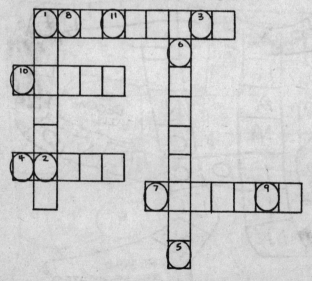

THE ___ ___ ___ ___   ___ ___ ___ ___ ___ ___ ___ .
     1   2   3   4   5   6   7   8   9 10 11

ABRAHAM LINCOLN WAS 1861 OUR 16TH PRESIDENT. LESS THAN SIX WEEKS AFTER HIS INAUGURAL ADDRESS, THE AMERICAN CIVIL WAR BEGAN. HE STOOD STRONG THROUGH THE FOUR YEARS OF WAR, AND WAS ABLE TO BRING THE NATION BACK TOGETHER. ON THE EVENING OF APRIL 14, 1865, WHAT MISFORTUNE HAPPENED TO "HONEST ABE"?

1865

FOLLOW THE CORRECT SPELLING OF THE NAME "ABRAHAM LINCOLN" TO THE CORRECT ANSWER.

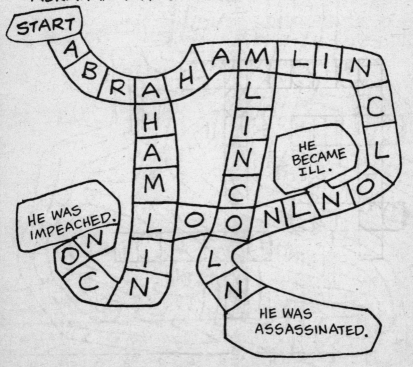

SEE ANSWER SECTION

ANDREW JOHNSON,
A MILITARY GOVERNOR
DURING THE CIVIL WAR,
BECAME OUR 17TH
PRESIDENT. HE WAS
THE FIRST PRESIDENT
TO BE ACCUSED AND
TRIED FOR MISBEHAVIOR.
WHOSE POLICIES DID
HE TRY TO FOLLOW WHILE
HE WAS IN OFFICE?

1865   1869

FOLLOW THIS MAZE TO THE CORRECT ANSWER.

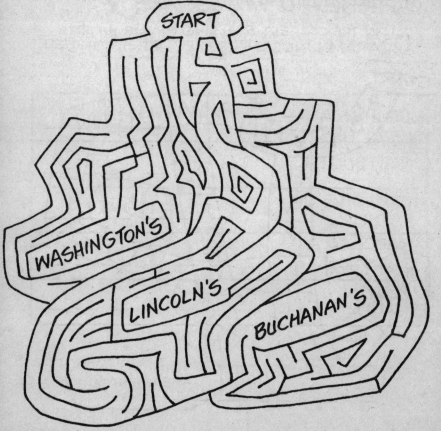

START

WASHINGTON'S

LINCOLN'S

BUCHANAN'S

SEE ANSWER SECTION

ULYSSES S. GRANT, OUR 18TH PRESIDENT, WAS THE COMMANDER OF THE UNION ARMY DURING THE CIVIL WAR. HE SERVED TWO TERMS IN OFFICE. AFTER HIS DEATH, WHAT FAMOUS AUTHOR PUBLISHED GRANT'S MEMOIRS?

1869   1877

WRITE THE ANSWER TO EACH CLUE IN THE SPACES. WRITE THE CIRCLED LETTERS, IN CORRECT NUMERICAL ORDER TO READ THE ANSWER.

Clue	Answer
GO FLY A —.	◯4 ◯8 _ _
NOT SOUTH.	◯9 _ ◯3 _
OPPOSITE OF FATHER.	◯1 _ ◯5 _
REPLY TO A QUESTION.	◯7 _ _ ◯6 _
RED FRUIT.	◯2 _ _ _ _

_1_ _2_ _3_ _4_

_5_ _6_ _7_ _8_ _9_

SEE ANSWER SECTION

RUTHERFORD B. HAYES WAS A SUCCESSFUL LAWYER BEFORE SERVING AS OUR 19TH PRESIDENT. DURING HIS TERM OF OFFICE, ALEXANDER GRAHAM BELL INVENTED THE TELEPHONE AND INSTALLED ONE IN THE WHITE HOUSE. WHY WAS HIS WIFE, LUCY, REFERRED TO AS "LEMONADE LUCY"?

1877 1881

USE THIS CHART TO DECODE THE ANSWER.

A	B	C	D	E	F	G	H	I	J	K	L	M
19	26	21	9	24	10	13	18	7	3	22	17	4

N	O	P	Q	R	S	T	U	V	W	X	Y	Z
12	16	2	23	11	15	8	25	1	6	20	5	14

26 24 21 19 25 15 24   15 18 24

11 24 10 25 15 24 9   8 16

15 24 11 1 24

19 17 21 16 18 16 17 7 21

9 11 7 12 22 15 .

1881

JAMES A. GARFIELD,
THE 20TH PRESIDENT,
WAS THE LAST PRESIDENT
TO BE RAISED IN A LOG
CABIN. HE WAS A
COMMANDER IN THE
UNION ARMY DURING
THE CIVIL WAR. HOW
WAS HIS PRESIDENTIAL
TERM CUT SHORT?

FILL IN THE MISSING LETTERS
WITH THEIR CORRECT VOWELS - A·E·I·O·U.

H__ W__S
SH__T __ND
K__LL__D BY __
D__S__PP____NT__D
J__B
S____K__R.

CHESTER ALAN ARTHUR
WAS OUR 21ST PRESIDENT.
HE WAS A FIGHTER FOR
CIVIL RIGHTS.
HE RAN A COMPLETELY
HONEST PRESIDENCY
AND WAS KNOWN AS
"THE GENTLEMAN BOSS."
WHICH FAMOUS BRIDGE
WAS COMPLETED
DURING HIS TERM?

1881   1885

CROSS OUT ALL THE LETTERS THAT
APPEAR 4 TIMES. WRITE THE REMAINING
LETTERS AS THEY APPEAR IN THE BLANK SPACES.

A	T	B	R	S
O	M	O	A	K
S	L	Y	T	M
N	B	S	R	M
T	I	D	T	G
A	S	M	E	A

THE

_ _ _ _ _ _ _ _

_ _ _ _ _ _ .

1885-1889   1893-1897

GROVER CLEVELAND SERVED AS OUR 22ND AND 23RD PRESIDENT. "HONESTY IS THE BEST POLICY" REPRESENTED HIS POLITICAL CAREER. WHAT WAS UNIQUE ABOUT HIS WIFE, FRANCES FOLSOM?

ANSWER EACH CLUE CORRECTLY AND WRITE THEM IN THE SPACES. WRITE THE CIRCLED LETTERS IN THEIR PROPER NUMERICAL ORDER TO READ THE ANSWER.

Clue	Answer (circled letter numbers)
OPPOSITE OF SUMMER.	_ (12) (3) _ _ (11)
RED, WHITE AND ___.	_ _ (16) (8)
___ STATES OF AMERICA.	(9) _ (4) _ _
FIVE PLUS THREE.	(2) _ (10) (6)
TRICK OR ___?	_ _ (13) (5) _ (15)
MIDDLE OF THE WEEK.	(1) _ (17) _ _ (14) _ (7)

AT T _ _ _ _ Y ON _ YEARS OF
    1 2 3 4   5

AGE, S _ E WAS THE
      6

_ O _ _ _ _ ST F _ _ _ _
7   8 9 10 11   12 13 14 15

_ A _ Y.
16 17

SEE ANSWER SECTION   23

BENJAMIN HARRISON, THE NATION'S 23RD PRESIDENT, WAS KNOWN AS "*THE MINORITY PRESIDENT.*" PRIOR TO BECOMING PRESIDENT HE WAS A LAWYER. WHICH NEW STATES WERE ADMITTED TO THE UNION DURING HIS TERM?

1889 1893

UNSCRAMBLE THE NAMES OF THESE SIX STATES.

WSAIHNTGNO
ANTNOMA
ONRHT OADKTA
OSTUH AKADOT
IADHO
OMYIWNG

24

SEE ANSWER SECTION

WILLIAM McKINLEY,
THE 25TH PRESIDENT,
DEALT WITH THE SPANISH-
AMERICAN WAR. AT THE
WARS END, THE U.S.
GAINED THE TERRITORIES
OF PUERTO RICO, THE
PHILIPPINES AND GUAM.
WHERE DID McKINLEY DO
HIS CAMPAIGNING FROM?

1897   1901

CIRCLE THE EVEN NUMBERED LETTERS AND
WRITE THEM AS THEY APPEAR IN THE BLANKS.

5 L	12 F	6 R	7 M	8 O	1 A
2 M	4 H	9 N	10 I	16 S	18 H
12 O	11 B	15 R	13 Q	8 M	7 K
1 H	10 E	16 I	4 N	3 E	18 C
2 A	5 R	12 N	6 T	20 O	21 Z
10 N	14 O	24 H	7 T	8 I	12 O

__ __ __ __   __ __ __

__ __ __ __ __ __

__ __ __ __ __ __ __ ,

__ __ __ __ __ .

SEE ANSWER SECTION

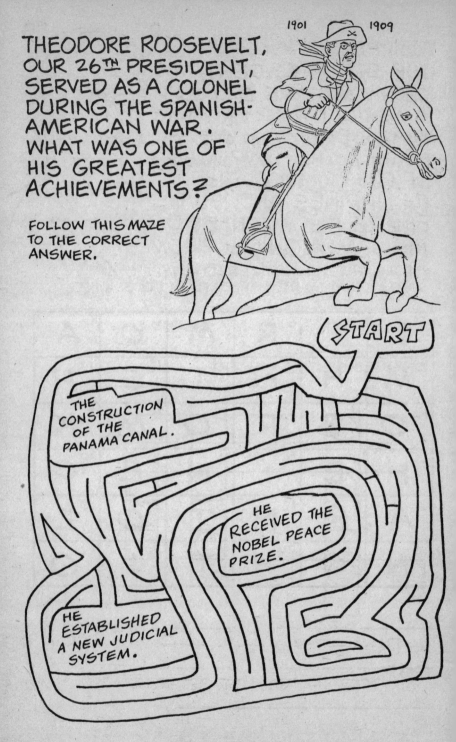

SEE ANSWER SECTION

WILLIAM HOWARD TAFT, OUR 27TH PRESIDENT, WAS KNOWN AS "BIG BILL." HE WAS THE FIRST PRESIDENT TO TAKE UP GOLF AND TO DRIVE AROUND WASHINGTON IN AN ELECTRIC CAR. BESIDES BEING PRESIDENT, WHAT OTHER HIGH GOVERNMENT OFFICE DID HE HOLD?

1909   1913

PLACE THESE WORDS IN THEIR CORRECT SPACES. WRITE THE CIRCLED LETTERS IN THEIR CORRECT NUMERICAL SPACES TO COMPLETE THE ANSWER.

COUNTRY • FREEDOM • MONUMENT • OFFICE • SERVE • TERM •

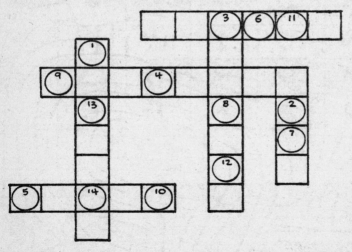

_ HI _ _ _ J _ _ T _ CE OF THE
  1 2 3   4 5 6

SUP _ _ _ _ _   _ _ _ _ T.
    7 8 9 10   11 12 13 14

SEE ANSWER SECTION   27

WOODROW WILSON, THE 28TH PRESIDENT WAS ONCE PRESIDENT OF PRINCETON UNIVERSITY. WHAT WAR STARTED AND ENDED DURING HIS ADMINISTRATION.

CROSS OUT THE LETTERS THAT HAVE A TRIANGLE △. WRITE THE REMAINING LETTERS, AS THEY APPEAR, IN THE BLANKS.

1913   1921

△N	△G	☆W	△H	△R
□O	○R	△T	□L	△C
△W	☆D	△I	○W	□A
△M	△D	○R	△S	△B
□O	△A	☆N	△F	☾E

___ ___ ___ ___ ___

___ ___ ___

___ ___ ___ .

SEE ANSWER SECTION

WARREN G. HARDING, THE 29TH PRESIDENT, CAMPAIGNED FROM THE FRONT PORCH OF HIS HOUSE IN OHIO. HIS PRESIDENTIAL QUALIFICATIONS WERE LACKING AND HIS OFFICE WAS ROCKED WITH SCANDALS. WHICH POLITICAL PARTY WAS HE WITH?

FILL IN THE AREAS THAT CONTAIN A DOT • TO FIND OUT.

SEE ANSWER SECTION

CALVIN COOLIDGE, OUR NATION'S 30TH PRESIDENT, WAS A QUIET AND SOLEMN MAN. CAUTIOUS AND FRUGAL, HE REDUCED THE NATIONAL DEBT BY TWO BILLION DOLLARS. AFTER HIS PRESIDENCY ENDED, WHAT DID HE DO?

1923
1929

USE THIS CHART TO DECODE THE ANSWER.

A	B	C	D	E	F	G	H	I	J	K	L	M
3	17	2	16	20	21	18	23	12	24	26	10	13

N	O	P	Q	R	S	T	U	V	W	X	Y	Z
7	4	1	25	8	9	14	11	15	6	22	5	19

—— —— —— —— —— —— —— ——
2   4   4   10   12   16   18   20

—— —— —— —— ——   ——
6   8   4   14   20   3

—— —— —— —— ——
16   3   12   10   5

—— —— —— —— —— —— —— —— ——
7   20   6   9   1   3   1   20   8

—— —— —— —— —— —— .
2   4   10   11   13   7

HERBERT HOOVER,
THE 31ST PRESIDENT,
WAS ONE OF THE WORLD'S
LEADING ENGINEERS.
WHILE PRESIDENT, THE
COUNTRY WAS HIT BY A
GREAT DEPRESSION.
WHAT ORGANIZATION
TRIED TO SAVE THE
NATION'S ECONOMY?

1929   1933

FOLLOW THE CORRECT PATH IN THIS
ALPHABET MAZE TO THE ANSWER.

START

THE RECONSTRUCTION FINANCE CORPORATION

THE BANK OF WASHINGTON

THE BANK COMPANY

SEE ANSWER SECTION

FRANKLIN D. ROOSEVELT, OUR 32ND PRESIDENT'S *"NEW DEAL"* BROUGHT LIFE BACK TO THE U.S. ECONOMY. HE WAS THE ONLY PRESIDENT TO SERVE MORE THAN TWO TERMS.

1933

1945

TO READ ONE OF ROOSEVELT'S FAMOUS QUOTATIONS, FILL IN THE BLANKS WITH THEIR CORRECT MISSING VOWELS A·E·I·O·U.

"TH__ __NLY
TH__NG W__
H__V__ T__
F____R __S
F____R
__TS__LF."

SEE ANSWER SECTION

HARRY S. TRUMAN
BECAME OUR 33RD
PRESIDENT WITHIN
FOUR HOURS AFTER
ROOSEVELT'S DEATH.
WORLD WAR TWO ENDED
UNDER HIS ADMINISTRATION.
NAME THE ORGANIZATION
THAT UNITED TWELVE
NATIONS TOGETHER TO
PRESERVE PEACE AND SECURITY.

1945   1953

WRITE THE OPPOSITE OF EACH WORD AND PLACE
THE CIRCLED LETTERS IN THEIR CORRECT NUMERICAL
SPACES TO COMPLETE THE ANSWER.

LEFT	◯ ◯ ◯ _ ◯
	3 15 13 8
HOT	◯ _ ◯ _
	7 6
SOUTH	◯ ◯ _ ◯ ◯
	1 12 11 4
QUESTION	◯ ◯ _ _ ◯ ◯
	5 14 10 9
FAST	_ _ ◯
	2

THE _ _ _ T _ _ T _ ANTI _
    1 2 3 4   5 6   7

_ _ _ A _ Y
8 9 10 11

_ R _ A _ IZAT _ ON.
12 13 14   15

SEE ANSWER SECTION

33

DWIGHT D. EISENHOWER, OUR 34TH PRESIDENT, WAS A FIVE STAR GENERAL DURING WORLD WAR TWO. HE SERVED AS PRESIDENT OF COLUMBIA UNIVERSITY AND WAS SUPREME COMMANDER OF NATO. WHAT WAS HIS NICKNAME?

FILL IN THE AREAS THAT HAVE A DOT • TO FIND OUT.

SEE ANSWER SECTION

JOHN F. KENNEDY,
OUR 35TH PRESIDENT,
WAS THE NATION'S FIRST
ROMAN CATHOLIC TO
BECOME PRESIDENT.
HE RECEIVED "THE
PURPLE HEART" MEDAL
FOR HIS INJURIES
RECEIVED IN W.W. II.
WHAT WAS HIS ADMINISTRATION
KNOWN AS?

CROSS OUT ALL THE A·C·J·M·S LETTERS.
WRITE THE REMAINING LETTERS, AS THEY APPEAR,
IN THE BLANKS.

1961 1963

J	N	A	E
W	F	C	M
S	R	O	N
A	T	S	J
I	C	E	R

THE ___ ___ ___

___ ___ ___ ___ ___ ___ ___ ___ .

SEE ANSWER SECTION

LYNDON B. JOHNSON, 1963 1969
OUR 36TH PRESIDENT,
WAS A LIEUTENANT
COMMANDER DURING
W.W.II, HOW DID
HE BECOME PRESIDENT?
FILL IN THE AREAS THAT HAVE A
DOT • TO FIND OUT

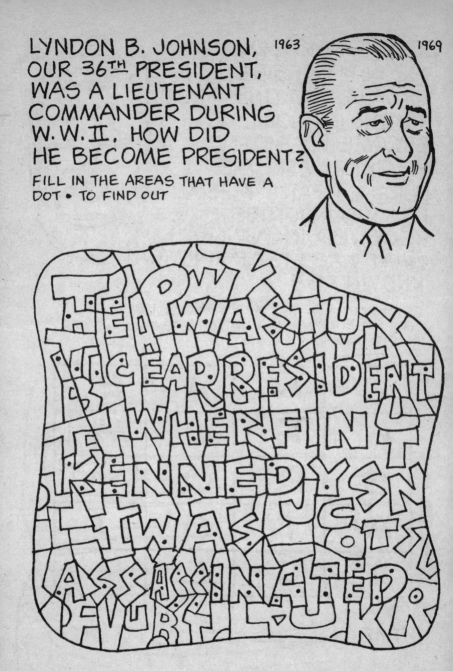

SEE ANSWER SECTION

RICHARD M. NIXON WAS OUR 37TH PRESIDENT. THE AMERICAN SPACE PROGRAM ACHIEVED GREAT SUCCESS DURING NIXON'S PRESIDENCY. WHO WAS HIS VICE PRESIDENT?

1969   1974

FOLLOW THIS MAZE TO THE CORRECT PRESIDENT.

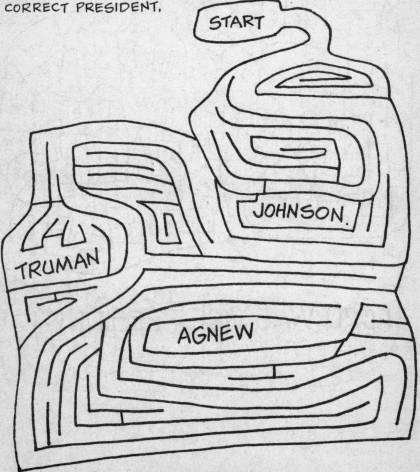

START

JOHNSON.

TRUMAN

AGNEW

SEE ANSWER SECTION

GERALD R. FORD
BECAME OUR 38TH
PRESIDENT IN A VERY
DIFFERENT WAY, HOW?

FILL IN THE AREAS THAT HAVE THE
LETTER "F" TO FIND OUT.

WHEN

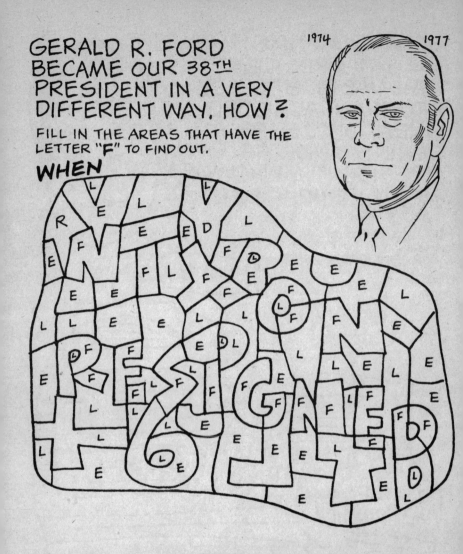

1974   1977

FORD WAS VICE PRESIDENT.

38

SEE ANSWER SECTION

JIMMY CARTER, OUR 39TH PRESIDENT, WAS THE FIRST PRESIDENT ELECTED FROM THE DEEP SOUTH SINCE BEFORE THE CIVIL WAR. WHAT WAS UNIQUE ABOUT HIS PRESIDENTIAL CABINET?

1977   1981

USE THIS CHART TO DECODE THE ANSWER.

A	B	C	D	E	F	G	H	I	J	K	L	M
7	15	14	12	9	21	24	10	6	26	20	23	13

N	O	P	Q	R	S	T	U	V	W	X	Y	Z
11	8	4	17	3	2	5	19	22	1	25	16	18

10 9   7 4 4 8 6 11 5 9 12

5 1 8   1 8 13 9 11

5 8   10 6 2

14 7 15 6 11 9 5 '

13 8 3 9   5 10 7 11

7 11 16   8 5 10 9 3

4 3 9 2 6 12 9 11 5 .

SEE ANSWER SECTION

RONALD REAGAN, OUR 40TH PRESIDENT, SERVED TWO TERMS AS GOVERNOR OF CALIFORNIA. HE WAS A FORMER FILM AND TV STAR. WHAT NAME IS GIVEN TO HIS ECONOMIC PLAN?

1981 –

UNSCRAMBLE THE NAMES OF THESE PRESIDENTS, WRITE THE CIRCLED LETTERS, IN NUMERICAL ORDER, TO READ THE ANSWER.

ALOTYR	___ (3) ___ (7) ___
ECREIP	___ (9) ___ ___ (2)
RANTG	(4)(1) ___ ___
HSYAE	___ (5) ___ (11)
CINLMKEY	(8)(10) ___ (6) ___

1' ‗ ‗ ‗ ‗ ‗ ‗ ‗ ‗ ‗ ‗ ‗ 11
   1 2 3 4 5 6 7 8 9 10 11

SEE ANSWER SECTION

STARTING WITH OUR FIRST PRESIDENT — HOW MANY OF THE 40 (REMEMBER ONE SERVED 2 SEPARATE TERMS) CAN YOU NAME ?

1-

2-

3-

4-

5-

6-

7-

8-

9-

10-

11-

12-

13-

14-

15-

16-

17-

18-

19-

20-

21-

22-

23-

24-

25-

26-

27-

28-

29-

30-

31-

32-

33-

34-

35-

36-

37-

38-

39-

40-

SEE ANSWER SECTION

NAME THE FIRST LADY WHO INTRODUCED ICE CREAM AT WHITE HOUSE FUNCTIONS.

CROSS OUT ALL THE ODD NUMBERED LETTERS. WRITE THE REMAINING LETTERS, AS THEY APPEAR, IN THE BLANK SPACES.

7 V	2 J	9 N	10 A	14 M	8 E
12 S	11 L	16 M	13 H	18 A	15 F
17 T	20 D	22 I	2 S	4 O	19 H
6 N	8 S	1 E	10 W	3 A	12 I
26 F	16 E	18 D	5 R	7 T	11 N
1 I	4 O	14 L	20 L	19 S	2 Y

__ __ __ __ __

__ __ __ __ __ __ ,

__ __ __ __

__ __ __ .

NAME THE PRESIDENT WHO CHOSE THE LOCATION FOR THE WHITE HOUSE AND THE CAPITOL.

COMPLETE THE CROSSWORD PUZZLE,
WRITE THE CIRCLED LETTERS AND UNSCRAMBLE
THEM TO LEARN THE ANSWER.

ACROSS:
1-NOT DRY
3-TO YELL
5-OPPOSITE OF WOMAN
6-MOVE QUICKLY

DOWN:
2-DAY BEFORE
   WEDNESDAY
4-WILD STRIPED
   CAT

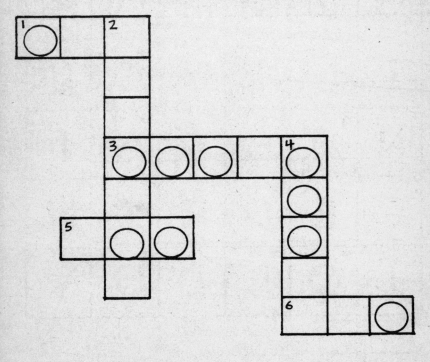

_____ _____ _____ _____ _____ _____ _____
SCRAMBLED LETTERS

_____ _____ _____ _____ _____ _____ _____
UNSCRAMBLED LETTERS

SEE ANSWER SECTION

DURING WOODROW WILSON'S ADMINISTRATION, HOW WAS THE LAWN OF THE WHITE HOUSE KEPT TRIM?

USE THIS CHART TO DECODE THE ANSWER.

A	B	C	D	E	F	G	H	I	J	K	L	M
9	17	4	15	1	24	5	25	7	14	23	22	10

N	O	P	Q	R	S	T	U	V	W	X	Y	Z
6	3	26	18	16	2	21	12	20	11	19	13	8

___ ___
17   13

___ ___ ___ ___ ___ ___ ___
5   16   9   8   7   6   5

___ ___ ___ ___ ___ ___
24   22   3   4   23   2

___ ___
3   24

___ ___ ___ ___ ___ .
2   25   1   1   26

44

SEE ANSWER SECTION

WHO WAS THE WIFE OF ONE PRESIDENT AND THE MOTHER OF ANOTHER?

CROSS OUT ALL THE LETTERS THAT APPEAR 6 TIMES. WRITE THE REMAINING LETTERS, AS THEY APPEAR, IN THE BLANK SPACES.

H	A	T	B	I	C
G	T	A	E	I	H
C	L	T	C	E	A
E	D	H	A	H	T
C	E	M	E	T	C
H	T	C	S	H	E

__ __ __ __ __ __ __

__ __ __ __ __

SEE ANSWER SECTION

WHO WAS THE OLDEST MAN TO BECOME PRESIDENT AT THE AGE OF 69 YEARS.

FOLLOW THE CORRECT PATH TO THE ANSWER.

START

THEODORE ROOSEVELT

BENJAMIN HARRIS

RONALD REAGAN

GROVER CLEVELAND

SEE ANSWER SECTION

WHAT WAS THE ORIGINAL COLOR OF THE WHITE HOUSE?

FILL IN THE AREAS THAT HAVE AN "X" TO FIND OUT.

SEE ANSWER SECTION

WHICH PRESIDENT DIED AFTER ONLY ONE MONTH IN OFFICE?

CIRCLE ALL THE LETTERS THAT CONTAIN A STAR ✹. WRITE THESE LETTER AS THEY APPEAR IN THE BLANK SPACES.

□ H	✹ W	○ E	✹ I	✹ L
✹ L	△ R	✹ I	✹ A	✹ M
✹ H	✹ E	✹ N	✹ R	△ L
○ I	✹ Y	□ G	○ W	✹ H
✹ A	△ D	✹ R	✹ R	△ K
✹ I	✹ S	○ R	✹ O	✹ N

___ ___ ___ ___ ___ ___ ___   ___ ___ ___ ___ ___

___ ___ ___ ___ ___ ___ ___ ___

SEE ANSWER SECTION

THE SEAL OF THE PRESIDENT OF THE UNITED STATES OF AMERICA.

WITHOUT LOOKING THROUGH THE BOOK, HOW MANY PRESIDENTS CAN YOU NAME AS THEY APPEAR ON THE NEXT TWO PAGES? WHEN YOU'VE FINISHED, TURN TO PAGE 64 TO CHECK YOUR ANSWERS.

1- _____

2- _____

3- _____

4- _____

SEE ANSWER SECTION

5-

6-

7-

8-

ANSWER SECTION

#3

#2

C I T Y H A L L
26 16 10 8 . 7 14 13 13

I N
16 23

N E W Y O R K .
23 4 25 8 17 12 21

THE ADAMS
FAMILY WAS
THE FIRST
FAMILY TO
LIVE IN THE
WHITE HOUSE.

#4

THE DAY AFTER MONDAY	T U E S D A Y
	5 · · 11 6 3 18
NOT LOUD	Q U I E T
	· · 14 1 10
SUMMER MONTH	A U G U S T
	12 17 · · 4
UNITED STATES OF _____	A M E R I C A
	15 13 · 8 2 · 7
FROZEN WATER	I C E
	· 16 9

THE DECIMAL SYSTEM OF
     1 2   3   4
DOLLARS AND CENTS USED IN
6 7 8   9 10 11
AMERICAN CURRENCY.
12 13   14 15   16 17   18

#5

BLOCK	B L A C K
	1
WHILE	W H I T E
	4 8 6
PINE	P I N K
	7 5
ROD	R E D
	3
GREED	G R E E N
	2 9

"FATHER OF THE
 1 2 3 4
CONSTITUTION"
 5 6 7 8 9

52

#6

#7

HIS FATHER
WAS THE
NATION'S
SECOND
PRESIDENT,
JOHN ADAMS.

#8

#9

X	D	A	X	X
V	X	Y	Y	C
X	R	X	X	O
C	X	K	X	X
X	X	X	E	X
X	T	X	X	T

DAVY
CROCKETT

E	V	A	R	B	L
E	W	I	N	M	A
C	A	O	R	R	R
A	L	E	K	E	E
E	T	B	E	D	D
P	O	W	E	R	E
G	A	L	F	O	F

"O.K."

53

#10

UP	(D)(O)(W)(N)
	8 4 7
COLD	(H)(O)(T)
	3 15 11
LEFT	(R)I(G)H(T)
	6 2
SIT	(S)(T)(A)(N)(D)
	9 13 1 14
SHORT	(T)A(L)(L)
	10 5 12

FOR HIS DEFE<u>AT</u> OF <u>HO</u>STI<u>L</u>E
<u>1/2</u>   <u>3 4</u>   5
<u>I N D</u>IAN<u>S</u> AT THE BA<u>T</u>T<u>L</u>E
6 7 8   9   10 11 12
OF <u>T</u>IPPECA<u>N</u><u>O</u>E RIVER.
   13   14 15

#11

T Y L E R
M A R R I E D
T W I C E A N D
H A D
F I F T E E N
C H I L D R E N .

#12

□ ✗	☆ M	○ E	□ ✗
☾ ✗	□ ✗	□ ✗	□ ✗
□ ✗	☼ I	☽ C	□ A
△ ✗	□ N	□ ✗	◇ W
○ A	□ ✗	○ R	□ ✗

THROUGH THE
<u>M E X I C A N</u>
<u>W A R</u>.

#13

START

GIVING A SPEECH AT THE WHITE HOUSE.

TRAVELING TO PHILADELPHIA

ATTENDING A CEREMONY FOR THE WASHINGTON MONUMENT.

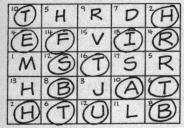

T	H	R	D	H
E	F	V	I	R
M	S	T	S	R
H	B	J	A	T
H	T	U	L	B

THE FIRST

BATHTUB.

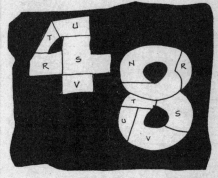

48

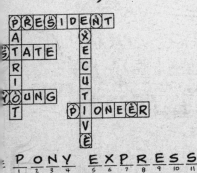

PRESIDENT
STATE   EXECUTIVE
PATRIOT
YOUNG
PIONEER

PONY EXPRESS.

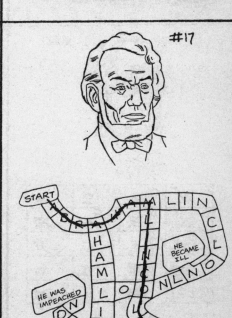

START

ABRAHAM LINCOLN
HAMLIN
HE BECAME ILL
HE WAS IMPEACHED
HE WAS ASSASSINATED

#18

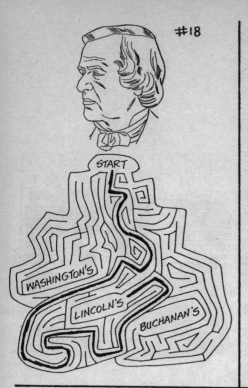

START

WASHINGTON'S

LINCOLN'S

BUCHANAN'S

#19

GO FLY A —.	(K) I T E
NOT SOUTH.	(N) O R T H
OPPOSITE OF FATHER.	(M) O T H E R
REPLY TO A QUESTION.	(A) N S W E R
RED FRUIT.	(A) P P L E

M A R K
T W A I N

#20

B E C A U S E   S H E

R E F U S E D   T O

S E R V E

A L C O H O L I C

D R I N K S.

#21

HE WAS
SHOT AND
KILLED BY A
DISAPPOINTED
JOB
SEEKER.

X̶	X̶	B	R	X̶
O	X̶	O	X̶	K
X̶	L	Y	X̶	M
N	B	X̶	R	X̶
X̶	I	D	X̶	G
X̶	X̶	X̶	E	X̶

THE
B R O O K L Y N
B R I D G E.

OPPOSITE OF SUMMER.	W I N T E R
	12 3 11
RED, WHITE AND —.	B L U E
	16 8
—— STATES OF AMERICA.	U N I T E D
	4
FIVE PLUS THREE.	E I G H T
	2 10 6
TRICK OR ——?	T R E A T
	13 15
MIDDLE OF THE WEEK.	W E D N E S D A Y
	1 17 14 7

AT T W E N T Y O N E YEARS OF
   1   2 3 4   5
AGE, S H E WAS THE
       6
Y O U N G E S T F I R S T
7   8 9 10 11   12 13 14 15
L A D Y.
16 17

NSAIHNTGNO	WASHINGTON
ANTNOMA	MONTANA
ONRHT OADKTA	NORTH DAKOTA
OSTUH AKADOT	SOUTH DAKOTA
IADHO	IDAHO
OMYIWNG	WYOMING

5 L	F	6 R	M	8 O	1 A
2 M	4 H	N	16 I	S	18 H
12 O	11 B	15 R	13 Q	M	7 K
1 H	10 E	16 I	4 N	3 E	18 C
2 A	5 R	12 N	22 O	21 Z	
19 N	14 O	24 H	7 T	17 I	

F R O M   H I S
H O M E   I N
C A N T O N
O H I O

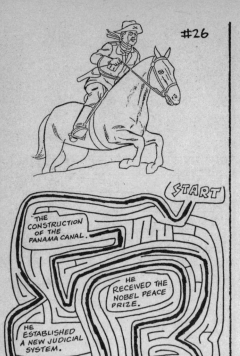

#26

THE CONSTRUCTION OF THE PANAMA CANAL.

HE RECEIVED THE NOBEL PEACE PRIZE.

HE ESTABLISHED A NEW JUDICIAL SYSTEM.

START

#27

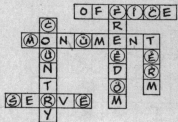

O F F I C E
F
C R E
M O N U M E N T
U D E
N O R
T M
R
S E R V E M

C H I E F   J U S T I CE   OF THE
1 2 3   4 5 6

SUP R E M E   C O U R T.
7 8 9 10   11 12 13 14

#28

❊ ❊ ☆W ❊ ❊
O R ❊ L ❊
❊ ☆D ❊ W A
❊ ❊ R ❊ ❊
O ❊ ☆N ❊ E

W O R L D
W A R
O N E.

#29

REPUBLICAN

58

#30

C O O L I D G E
2 4 4 10 12 16 18 20

W R O T E   A
6 8 4 14 20   3

D A I L Y
16 3 12 10 5

N E W S P A P E R
7 20 6 9 1 3 1 20 8

C O L U M N .
2 4 10 11 13 7

#31

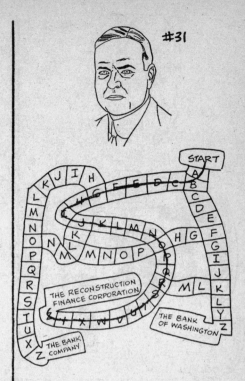

START

THE RECONSTRUCTION FINANCE CORPORATION

THE BANK OF WASHINGTON

THE BANK COMPANY

#32

"THE ONLY
THING WE
HAVE TO
FEAR IS
FEAR
ITSELF."

#33

LEFT	R I G H T
	3 15 13 8
HOT	C O L D
	7 6
SOUTH	N O R T H
	1 12 11 4
QUESTION	A N S W E R
	5 14 10 9
FAST	S L O W
	2

THE N O R T H   A T L A N T I C
     1 2 3 4   5 6   7

T R E A T Y
8 9 10 11

O R G A N I Z A T I O N .
12 13 14   15

#34

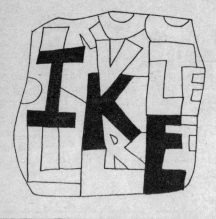

#35

⊠	N	⊠	E
W	F	⊠	⊠
⊠	R	O	N
⊠	T	⊠	⊠
I	⊠	E	R

THE <u>N E W</u>
<u>F R O N T I E R</u>.

#36

#37

#38

#39

WHEN

FORD WAS VICE PRESIDENT.

HE APPOINTED
10 9   7 4 4 8 6 11 5 9 12

TWO WOMEN
5 1 8   1 8 13 9 11

TO HIS
5 8   10 6 2

CABINET.
14 7 15 6 11 9 5

MORE THAN
13 8 3 9   5 10 7 11

ANY OTHER
4 3 9   2 6 12 9 3

PRESIDENT.
4 3 9 2 6 12 9 11 5

#40

ALOTVR	T A Y L O R
	3 7
ECREIP	P I E R C E
	9 2
RANTG	G R A N T
	4 1
HSYAE	H A Y E S
	5 11
CINLMKEY	M C K I N L E Y
	8 10 6

"R E A G A N O M I C S"
1 2 3 4 5 6 7 8 9 10 11

61

1- GEORGE WASHINGTON	21- CHESTER A. ARTHUR
2- JOHN ADAMS	22- GROVER CLEVELAND
3- THOMAS JEFFERSON	23- BENJAMIN HARRISON
4- JAMES MADISON	24- GROVER CLEVELAND
5- JAMES MONROE	25- WILLIAM McKINLEY
6- JOHN QUINCY ADAMS	26- THEODORE ROOSEVELT
7- ANDREW JACKSON	27- WILLIAM HOWARD TAFT
8- MARTIN VAN BUREN	28- WOODROW WILSON
9- WILLIAM HENRY HARRISON	29- WARREN G. HARDING
10- JOHN TYLER	30- CALVIN COOLIDGE
11- JAMES K. POLK	31- HERBERT HOOVER
12- ZACHARY TAYLOR	32- FRANKLIN D. ROOSEVELT
13- MILLARD FILLMORE	33- HARRY S. TRUMAN
14- FRANKLIN PIERCE	34- DWIGHT D. EISENHOWER
15- JAMES BUCHANAN	35- JOHN F. KENNEDY
16- ABRAHAM LINCOLN	36- LYNDON B. JOHNSON
17- ANDREW JOHNSON	37- RICHARD M. NIXON
18- ULYSSES S. GRANT	38- GERALD R. FORD
19- RUTHERFORD B. HAYES	39- JIMMY CARTER
20- JAMES A. GARFIELD	40- RONALD REAGAN

#42

7 ☒	2 J	9 ☒	10 A	14 M	8 E
12 S	11 ☒	16 M	13 ☒	18 A	15 ☒
17 ☒	20 D	22 I	2 S	4 O	19 ☒
6 N	8 S	1 ☒	10 W	3 ☒	12 I
26 F	16 E	18 D	5 ☒	7 ☒	11 ☒
1 ☒	4 O	14 L	20 L	19 ☒	2 Y

JAMES
MADISON'S
WIFE
DOLLY.

#43

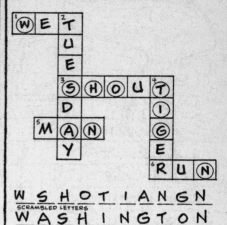

WSHOTIANGN
SCRAMBLED LETTERS
WASHINGTON
UNSCRAMBLED LETTERS

#44

BY
17 13

GRAZING
5 16 9 8 7 6 5

FLOCKS
24 22 3 4 23 2

OF
3 24

SHEEP.
2 25 1 1 26

#45

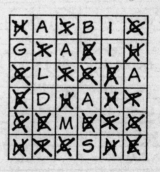

ABIGAIL
ADAMS

#46

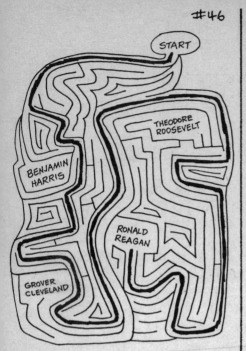

START

THEODORE ROOSEVELT

BENJAMIN HARRIS

RONALD REAGAN

GROVER CLEVELAND

#47

#48

WILLIAM HENRY HARRISON

#50-51

1-JAMES MADISON
2-GEORGE WASHINGTON
3-ABRAHAM LINCOLN
4-ULYSSES S. GRANT
5-THOMAS JEFFERSON
6-THEODORE ROOSEVELT
7-DWIGHT D. EISENHOWER
8-JOHN F. KENNEDY